DATE DUE

DISCARD

GAYLORD   PRINTED IN U.S.A.

Teach Me...™ Everyday
ITALIAN
Volume 2
Celebrating the Seasons

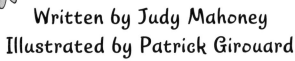

Written by Judy Mahoney
Illustrated by Patrick Girouard

Our mission at Teach Me... to enrich children through language learning.

The *Teach Me Everyday* series of books introduces common words, phrases and concepts to the beginning language learner through delightful songs and story. These engaging books are designed with an audio CD, encouraging children to read, listen and speak. *Teach Me Everyday Volume 2* celebrates the seasons and activities throughout the year. Follow Marie and her family as they venture out to the zoo, go on a picnic, visit museums, build a snowman and celebrate the holidays. The text is presented in a dual language learning format, meaning the Italian and English are side by side in order to enhance understanding and increase retention. The audio is narrated in Italian and introduces music memory through familiar songs. Children of all ages will enjoy exploring new languages as they sing and learn with *Teach Me*.

The Italian language is unique in that it is spoken primarily in one country, Italy. Children will enjoy learning Italian because almost 40 percent of Italian words are similar to their English equivalent. In addition, many Italian words are part of our English vocabulary already, such as pizza, ravioli, spaghetti, gondola and bambino. And notice that most Italian words end in a vowel!

Teach Me Everyday Italian – Volume 2: Celebrating the Seasons
ISBN 13: 978-1-59972-207-8 (library binding)
Library of Congress Control Number: 2008902659

Copyright © 2009 by Teach Me Tapes Inc.
6016 Blue Circle Drive, Minnetonka, MN 55343 USA
www.teachmeinc.com

With respect to the differences in language, the translations provided are not literal.

Book design by The Design Lab, Northfield, Minnesota.
Compact discs are replicated in the United States of America in Maple Grove, Minnesota.

Printed in the United States of America in North Mankato, Minnesota.
092009
08212009

1 0 9 8 7 6 5 4 3 2

INDEX & SONG LIST

LA PRIMAVERA
SPRING

L'ESTATE
SUMMER

L'AUTUNNO
AUTUMN

L'INVERNO
WINTER

Tu canterai, io canterò

Tu canterai, io canterò, noi canteremo insieme
Tu canterai, io canterò, se fa bello o piove
Tu canterai, io canterò, noi canteremo insieme
Tu canterai, io canterò, se fa bello o piove.

You'll Sing a Song
You'll sing a song and I'll sing a song
And we'll sing a song together
You'll sing a song and I'll sing a song
In warm or wintry weather.

la giraffa
giraffe

Andiamo allo zoo

Mamma ci porta allo zoo domani, zoo domani, zoo domani
Mamma ci porta allo zoo domani, per tutto il mattin.
Noi andiamo allo zoo, zoo, zoo, perchè anche tu, tu, tu?
Non vieni con me, me, me, andiamo allo zoo, zoo, zoo.

Guarda la scimmia saltare tra i rami...
Guarda nell' acqua nuotare il coccodrillo...

la scimmia
monkey

l'asino
donkey

il leone
lion

Going to the Zoo
Momma's taking us to the zoo tomorrow
Zoo tomorrow, zoo tomorrow
Momma's taking us to the zoo tomorrow
We can stay all day.

We're going to the zoo, zoo, zoo
How about you, you, you?
You can come too, too, too
We're going to the zoo, zoo, zoo.

Look at all the monkeys swinging in the trees...
Look at all the crocodiles swimming in the water...

nove

Il gioco di "Il mago dice"
Il mago dice: "Mettete la mano destra sulla testa!"
Il mago dice: "Toccate terra!"
Il mago dice: "Marciate!"
Il mago dice: "Applaudite!"
Il mago dice: "Dite il vostro nome!"
          "Maria, Francesco, Angela"
"Ridete forte!"... "Il mago non l'ha detto!"

Simon Says Game
Simon says: "Put your right hand on your head!"
Simon says: "Touch the ground!"
Simon says: "Walk!"
Simon says: "Clap your hands!"
Simon says: "Say your name!"
          "Marie, Francesco, Angela"
"Laugh out loud"..."Simon did not say!"

il cane
dog

Dopo la primavera viene l'estate. D'estate noi andiamo alla spiaggia. Io porto la palla e la barchetta.

After spring comes summer. In the summer we go to the beach. I bring my beach ball and toy boat.

I bring my sand pail and shovel to the beach.

Alla spiaggia porto il mio secchiello e la paletta.

Medoro! Non li distruggere!

Medoro! Don't destroy them!

Mettiamo il costume da bagno e facciamo dei bei castelli di sabbia.

We put on our swimsuits and make beautiful castles in the sand.

la sabbia
sand

la barchetta
boat

la palla
ball

La barchetta in mezzo al mare

La barchetta in mezzo al mare
È diretta a Sante Fè
Dove deve caricare
Mezzo chilo di caffè
La comanda un capitano
Dalla barba rossa e blu
Viene molto da lontano
Nientemen che dal Perù.

Santa Lucia

Sul mare luccica
L'astro d'argento
Placida è l'onda
Prospero è il vento.

Venite all'agile
Barchetta mia
Santa Lucia
Santa Lucia.

The Little Boat

The little boat in the middle of the sea
Is directed to Santa Fe
Where it must load
Half a kilo of coffee
The captain in command
Has a red and blue beard
He comes from far away
As far as from Peru.

Santa Lucia

The silver star
Glitters on the ocean
Calm is the wave
Fair is the wind.

Come to
My nimble little boat
Santa Lucia
Santa Lucia.

'O sole mio
Che bella cosa 'na jurnata 'e sole
N'aria serena dopo 'na tempesta!
Pe' l'aria fresca pare già 'na festa
Che bella cosa 'na jurnata 'e sole.

Mannat'u sole, chiù bello 'i me
'O sole mio sta in fronte a te!
'O sole, sole mio
Sta in fronte a te, sta in fronte a te!

'O Sole Mio
What a beautiful thing a sunny day
The serene air after the storm!
For the fresh air it seems already a feast
What a beautiful thing a sunny day.

Sunny day, more beautiful you are
My sunshine is in front of you!
Sunshine, my sunshine
Is in front of you, is in front of you!

Più tardi attraversiamo la strada per andare al museo d'arte.

Later we cross the street to go to the art museum.

Guarda i quadri di Van Gogh. I girasoli nei suoi quadri sembrano quelli nel mio giardino.

Mi piace guardare i tori nei quadri di Goya. Io faccio finta di essere il torero.

Look at the paintings of Van Gogh. The sunflowers in his painting look like those in my garden.

I like to look at the bulls in the paintings by Goya. I pretend to be the matador.

Casimiro
Casimiro, vieni asinello vien
Casimiro, vieni asinello vien
Asinello svelto, asinello lento
L'asinello viene, l'asinello va
Asinello svelto, asinello lento
L'asinello viene, l'asinello va.

Tingalayo
Tingalayo, come little donkey come
Tingalayo, come little donkey come
Me donkey fast, me donkey slow
Me donkey come and me donkey go
Me donkey fast, me donkey slow
Me donkey come and me donkey go.

After summer comes autumn.
The leaves turn yellow.
I gather leaves,
chestnuts and grapes.

Dopo l'estate viene l'autunno.
Le foglie diventano gialle.
Io raccolgo le foglie,
le castagne e l'uva.

lo scoiattolo
squirrel

le castagne
chestnuts

Reginella campagnola
Tra la la la la la...

All' alba quando spunta il sole
Là nell'Abruzzo tutto d'or
Le prosperose campagnole
Discendono le valli in fior.

O campagnola bella
Tu sei la reginella
Negli occhi tuoi c'è il sole
C'è il colore delle viole
Delle valli tutte in fior!

Se canti la tua voce
È un'armonia di pace
Che si diffonde e dice
"Se vuoi vivere felice
Devi vivere quassù!"

Oh, Country Girl
Tra la la la la la...

At dawn when the sun rises
There in the all golden Abruzzo
The country girls
Come down the valleys in bloom.

Oh, beautiful country girl
You are the little queen
In your eyes there is the sunshine
There is the color of the violets
Of the valleys all in bloom!

If you sing, your voice
Is a harmony of peace
Which expands and says
"If you want to live happy
You must live up here!"

diciannove

19

il nostro nonno
our grandpa

il cereale
corn

Prima di tornare a scuola andiamo alla fattoria del nonno. Diamo da mangiare alle mucche, ai polli ed ai maialini.

Mio nonno tosa le pecore. Più tardi ci porta in giro sul trattore con i nostri cugini.

Before returning to school we visit Grandpa's farm. We feed the cows, chickens and pigs.

My Grandpa shears the sheep. Later he takes us on a tractor ride with our cousins.

Alla fattoria del nonno
Su andiamo, su andiamo
Alla fattoria del nonno
Su andiamo, su andiamo
Alla fattoria del nonno.

Alla fattoria del nonno c'è una vacca bruna (bis)
La vacca ha fatto un vitellino: Mu! (bis)

Alla fattoria del nonno c'è una gallinella (bis)
La gallina ha fatto un bel pulcino: Pio! Pio! (bis)

Down on Grandpa's Farm
Oh, we're on our way, we're on our way
On our way to Grandpa's farm
We're on our way, we're on our way
On our way to Grandpa's farm.

Down on Grandpa's farm there is a big brown cow (repeat)
The cow, she makes a sound like this: Moo! (repeat)

Down on Grandpa's farm there is a little red hen (repeat)
The hen, she makes a sound like this: Cluck! Cluck! (repeat)

l'agnello
lamb

Agnellino bianco

Agnellino bianco hai un po' di lana?
Sì signore, sì signore, tre sacchi pieni
Uno per Lei, l'altro per la dama
Uno pel bambino, che vive un po' più in là.

Baa Baa Black Sheep
Baa baa black sheep have you any wool?
Yes sir, yes sir, three bags full
One for my master and one for my dame
One for the little boy who lives down the lane.

i polli
chickens

la mucca
cow

Nella vecchia fattoria

Nella vecchia fattoria, ia – ia – oh
Quante bestie ha zio Tobia, ia – ia – oh
C'è una mucca mu, mucca mu
Mucca, mucca, mucca mu
Nella vecchia fattoria, ia – ia – oh.

C'è un cane bau, cane bau, cane, cane, cane bau...
C'è un gatto miao, gatto miao, gatto, gatto, gatto miao...
C'è un maiale gru, maiale gru, maiale, maiale, maiale gru...

Old MacDonald
Old MacDonald had a farm, E - I - E - I - O
And on his farm he had a cow, E - I - E - I - O
With a cow moo here, and a cow moo there
Here a moo, there a moo, everywhere a moo, moo
Old MacDonald had a farm, E - I - E - I – O.

With a dog bark here, and a dog bark there...
With a cat meow here, and a cat meow there...
With a pig snort here, and a pig snort there...

Stasera festeggiamo Halloween con i nostri amici americani. Ora intagliamo una zucca.

Tonight we celebrate Halloween with our American friends. I carve a face on a pumpkin.

la zucca
pumpkin

Cinque piccole zucche

Cinque piccole zucche sedute sul muretto.
La prima dice: "Cielo, fa freschetto!"
La seconda dice: "Le streghe son nel vento."
La terza dice: "Io non mi spavento."
La quarta dice: "Dobbiamo presto partire."
La quinta dice: "Oh no! Mi voglio divertire."
"Huuh-Huuh" dice il vento. La luce se ne va
E le zucche fuggono di qua e di là.

Five Little Pumpkins

Five little pumpkins sitting on a gate.
The first one said, "Oh my, it's getting late!"
The second one said, "There are witches in the air."
The third one said, "But we don't care."
The fourth one said, "Let's run and run and run."
The fifth one said, "I'm ready for some fun."
"Oo-oo" went the wind, and out went the light
And the five little pumpkins rolled out of sight.

la neve
snow

Guarda, cade la neve!
Andiamo a giocare sulla neve!
Tiriamo le slitte sulla collina
e ci lanciamo giù.

Look, snow is falling!
Let's play in the snow!
We pull our sleds up the hill
and we slide down.

Poi facciamo un grandissimo
pupazzo di neve. Ha gli occhi di
carbone, per naso una carota, porta
un cappello a bombetta e la sciarpa
della mia mamma.

Then we will
build a huge snowman.
He has coal eyes, a carrot
nose, wears a derby hat
and my mother's scarf.

il pupazzo di neve
snowman

Il pupazzo di neve

È un mio amico
Lo conosci tu
Porta la bombetta
È freddo come il ghiaccio.

Ha occhi di carbone
Per naso una carota
Le braccia di bastone
E un manto di neve.

Indovini il suo nome?
Ascolta cosa dico
Non si vede mai
Eccetto che d'inverno.

Indovina! Chi è?
Chi è? Indovina!
Chi è?
È il pupazzo di neve!

Snowman Song
There's a friend of mine
You might know him too
Wears a derby hat
He's real cool.

He has coal black eyes
An orangy carrot nose
Two funny stick-like arms
And a snowy overcoat.

Have you guessed his name?
Or do you need a clue
You'll never see his face
In autumn, summer, spring.

Guess! Who is it?
Who is it? Guess!
Who is it?
It's the snowman!

Din don dan

Din don dan, din don dan, che felicità!
Sulla slitta tutti siam e di gioia noi cantiamo!
Din don dan, din don dan, che felicità!
Sulla slitta tutti siam e di gioia noi cantiam!

Com'è bello andar
Sulla slitta insieme a te
Con tanta neve che
Dal cielo scende giù
Tintinnando va il nostro cavallin
E insieme noi cantiamo
Buona notte, buon Natal.

Jingle Bells

Jingle bells, jingle bells
Jingle all the way!
Oh what fun it is to ride
In a one-horse open sleigh, hey!

Dashing through the snow
In a one-horse open sleigh
O'er the fields we go
Laughing all the way
Bells on bob-tail ring
Making spirits bright
What fun it is to laugh and sing
A sleighing song tonight!

Santa Notte

Bianco Natal, notte d'amor
Tutto tace, il cielo è d'or
Bianca splende la luna nel ciel
Gloria cantano gli angeli in ciel
Nella notte divina
Nato è il Bambino Gesù.

Silent Night

Silent night, holy night
All is calm, all is bright
'Round yon Virgin, Mother and Child
Holy infant, so tender and mild
Sleep in heavenly peace
Sleep in heavenly peace.

It is time for the holidays. We celebrate
Christmas and prepare the
nativity. We also bake
cookies and decorate our house.
We sing Christmas songs.

Sono le feste. Noi celebriamo la festa di Natale e facciamo il Presepio. Facciamo anche dei biscotti e decoriamo la casa. Cantiamo canzoni natalizie.

i biscotti cookies

il palloncino
balloon

Noi sappiamo i mesi dell'anno! Voi li sapete?

Now we know the months of the year. Do you?

gennaio	January
febbraio	February
marzo	March
aprile	April
maggio	May
giugno	June
luglio	July
agosto	August
settembre	September
ottobre	October
novembre	November
dicembre	December

Teach Me...
VOCABOLARIO
Vocabulary

LA PRIMAVERA
SPRING

ciao	hello
il giardino	garden
le verdure	vegetables
i fiori	flowers
il leone	lion
la giraffa	giraffe
la scimmia	monkey
il compleanno	birthday
la festa	party
la torta	cake
il gioco	game

L'ESTATE
SUMMER

la spiaggia	beach
la paletta	shovel
il secchiello	pail
il costume da bagno	bathing suit
la sabbia	sand
le nuvole	clouds
la barca	boat
il formaggio	cheese
la banana	banana
il pane	bread
le formiche	ants

L'AUTUNNO
AUTUMN

le castagne	chestnuts
il gatto	cat
il cane	dog
l'albero	tree
il rastrello	rake
la fattoria	farm
la pecora	sheep
la mucca	cow
le zucche	pumpkins
il lupo	wolf

L'INVERNO
WINTER

la slitta	sled
il pupazzo di neve	snowman
la carota	carrot
la sciarpa	scarf
la notte	night
buon anno	Happy New Year
la caramella	candy
la mascherina	mask
i miei amici	my friends
arrivederci	goodbye